Immersed in Grace

Church Times Study Guide

Immersed in Grace

Exploring Baptism

Stephen Burns

CANTERBURY
PRESS
Norwich

First published in 2005 by the Canterbury Press Norwich
(a publishing imprint of Hymns Ancient &
Modern Limited, a registered charity)
St Mary's Works, St Mary's Plain,
Norwich, Norfolk, NR3 3BH

www.scm-canterburypress.co.uk

British Library Cataloguing in Publication data

A catalogue record for this book is available
from the British Library

ISBN 1-85311-686-6
978-185311-686-5

Typeset by Regent Typesetting, London
Printed and bound in Great Britain by Gallpen Colour Print,
Norwich 01603 624893

Contents

Introduction: Images of Baptism   vii

1   Baptism and the Richness of Scripture   1
2   Baptism and the Journey of Faith   5
3   Baptism and the Church's Mission   9
4   Baptism and Christian Spirituality   14

Conclusion   18
References and Further Reading   20

Introduction

Images of Baptism

What does it mean to us that we are baptized? What does it mean to us together to be the *community of the baptized?* Is baptism something that happened to us a long time ago, or a marker of our basic Christian identity?

There are many possible answers to these questions, and some are demonstrated in the following images. Baptism matters in all of them. Each is powerful, touching human highs or lows, celebrations or crises. For a moment or so, imagine them with me.

First, get caught up in a procession from Omsk Cathedral to a nearby lake for the Orthodox ceremony that accompanies 'the Theophany', an event in the liturgical calendar that corresponds to the Baptism of Christ in the Epiphany season of western churches. It is just after the end of Communist rule, and you witness the most extraordinary sight: first a deacon wades into the water, 'deeper and deeper . . . while his vestments fanned out over the surface, their mauve silk waterlogged into indigo, while he was spread below like an outlandish bird over the pool'. He traces the sign of the cross on the water, while the archbishop scoops up water from the lake in a chalice and ceremonially sprinkles it back in again. The procession then leaves, though countless 'babushkas' (mainly elderly women) stay at the lake's edge. As if to redress the suppression of their religion under the former rule, they proceed to peel off their clothes and wade right in. 'They plunge mountainously in . . . shouting and jubilant . . . cradle water in their hands and dash it off their faces.' They drink, they fill empty cola bottles with the newly-blessed lake-water, 'they slosh its torrent exultantly over one another' (Thubron, *In Siberia*, pp. 55–7). These extravagant gestures of freedom, of celebration, are, for them, linked with the memory of Jesus' baptism, as well as recalling their own. The merriment centres on God's affirmation of his well-pleasing beloved one.

Imagine next an urban hospital. It is night-time, the room is subdued, and distraught parents are holding in their arms their newborn child. She has died. The chaplain gently wipes tears from the parents' exhausted faces and smears the tears over the lifeless child they are cradling, saying: 'Baby, I baptize you in the name of the Father, and of the Son and the Holy Spirit.'

Patton, *From Ministry to Theology*, p. 1

Then travel back in time – to the late fourth-century – for our third image. 'Shiver in the cold of early Easter morning and with awe at what is about to transpire.' See the bishop command the proceedings concerning the 'catechumens' – seekers after Christian truth, engaged in learning the faith over time. This is the night when they will be baptized. They strip, face westwards to the dying sun and denounce the 'king of shadows'. Their bodies are rubbed with olive oil, they receive prayer and are quizzed about their understanding of their faith. Then they are led, one by one, to a pool of water. Standing in the pool, each catechumen is asked 'Do you believe . . . ?' [in the Father, the Son and the Holy Spirit] and immediately following an affirmative answer is plunged beneath the water. Breathless, stepping back out on to the side, each is oiled once more – this time with richly fragranced perfume – is given an oil-lamp and led in procession to meet the dawn: 'tired, damp, thrilled and oily – out into the blaze of Easter morning'. In the light, they are greeted by the ovations of the assembled church, embraced and fed for the first time at eucharist (Kavanagh, 'A Rite of Passage', pp. 171–5). As we shall see, extraordinary accounts of early baptisms, like this, are important to how churches are re-conceiving baptism in our own times.

These images might be hard to imagine, at least for some of us, and they probably bear little resemblance to memories of our own baptism

– if we can remember it – or that of others, for they are not likely to be like baptism as it has happened recently in our local church. But the crucial point is that baptism matters in these stories: it signifies something important, even vital, in the lives of the people who feature in them. The stories place baptism in the midst of joy, pain, glory, endurance, intimacy, awe. Baptism is close to the heart of the Siberians' liberation, it aches alongside those wrecked parents, it confronts the catechumens' choices about ways to live, what to believe, whose company to keep.

This study aims to help us recover a sense of excitement about baptism, and to offer some clues about how baptism might find more central significance in the life of the church community. It affirms that baptism shapes the core of Christian identity and invites radical faith. It trusts that baptism has relevance to every circumstance of our lifelong journey, and it invites and challenges a lively sense of what it means to be baptized. In this study we will think about three related and overlapping categories:

- Baptism and the journey of faith.
- Baptism and the church's mission.
- Baptism and Christian spirituality.

In preparation it might be helpful to read through the service of Holy Baptism in *Common Worship*. You will find it on pages 344–73.

Exercise

Recall your own baptism, or your most recent experiences of baptismal celebrations. Compare them with these stories.

1

Baptism and the Richness of Scripture

Jesus is at the heart of Christian baptism: the gospels remember him being baptized as the occasion on which he was affirmed as God's own beloved (Mark 1.9–11; Matthew 3.13–17; Luke 3.21–22; also John 1.29–34) and recall him speaking of his passion as a baptism (Mark 10.38; Luke 12.50). Matthew includes a post-resurrection narrative in which the risen one instructs others to teach and baptize (Matthew 28.19–20). John's gospel also contains a hint of disagreement about whether or not Jesus himself baptized, earlier in his ministry, if not later. Compare these two versions:

After this Jesus and his disciples went into the Judean countryside, and he spent some time there with them and baptized (John 3.22).

Although it was not Jesus himself but his disciples who baptized (John 4.2).

The later seems deliberately to cancel out the ambiguity of the former.

Other New Testament scriptures cite the name of Jesus at the heart of others' baptism, for example:

Peter said to them 'Repent and be baptized every one of you in the name of Jesus Christ so that your sins may be forgiven; and you will receive the gift of the Holy Spirit (Acts 2.38).

But when they believed Philip, who was proclaiming the good news about the kingdom of God and the name of Jesus Christ, they were baptized, both men and women (Acts 8.12).

On hearing this, they were baptized in the name of the Lord Jesus (Acts 19.5).

So he ordered them to be baptized in the name of Jesus Christ. Then they invited him to stay for several days (Acts 44.48).

Their response to him is the reason for their submitting to the waters.

In the manifold New Testament accounts of people being baptized, particularly in Acts, there is a chaos about when and how they were baptized. They were sometimes responding to prior animation by the Holy Spirit, sometimes baptized without consciousness of divine presence and blessing, and sometimes subject to the laying on of hands by Christian leaders somewhere along the way of coming to belong among the Christian people. Sometimes people first came to belief and then were baptized, and at other times they brought their 'households' to the waters as part of their individual response to the good news. Perhaps they sometimes brought their children, perhaps as part of the whole household being baptized.

One way to read the differences within the scriptural witness to baptism is as testimony to the utter sovereignty of God, whose mercy overflows uniform patterns or rigid understanding: baptism happened among new believers and those who mattered to them as the liberating Spirit refused for grace to be ordered by any restrictive criteria!

It can be helpful at this point to consider a World Council of Churches report that identifies some of the characteristics common to both adult and child baptism:

- they both 'take place in the community of faith';
- they both are 'rooted in and declare Christ's faithfulness unto death';
- in both, 'the baptized person will have to grow in understanding of faith';
- and both 'require a similar and responsible attitude towards Christian nurture'.

Baptism, Eucharist and Ministry, Baptism, p. 12

Reflecting the Bible's stories of people being baptized in different circumstances, *Common Worship*'s service of baptism is quite consciously designed for use with both adults and children.

Just as the scriptures suggest a range of *practice* concerning baptism in the early Christian communities, so they also indicate a range of theological *understandings*. Various New Testament writers accent different images, metaphors and symbols to unfold baptismal meaning. Most of the key biblical meanings are spelled out in *Baptism, Eucharist and Ministry*, which is the basis for a great deal of ecumenical convergence in recent decades: it highlights the meanings of baptism as:

- participation in Christ's death and resurrection (Romans 6.3–5; Colossians 2.12);
- a washing away of sin (1 Corinthians 6.11);
- a new birth (John 3.5);
- an enlightenment by Christ (Ephesians 5.14);
- a reclothing in Christ (Galatians 3.27);
- a renewal by the Spirit (Titus 3.5);
- an experience of salvation from the flood (1 Peter 3.20–21);
- an exodus from bondage (1 Corinthians 10.1–2);
- a liberation into a new humanity in which barriers of division whether of sex or race or social status are transcended (Galatians 3.27–28; 1 Corinthians 12.13).

Baptism, Eucharist and Ministry concludes that 'the images are many but the reality is one' (BEM Baptism, 12).

Over time, two images in particular came to have particular influence on the church's tradition of baptism: the idea of baptism as 'new birth', rooted in John 3.1–15, and the idea of baptism as a kind of death, rooted in Romans 6.1–14. But the rich diversity of images to be found in the New Testament is in part responsible for the variety of symbols that are often present in the celebration of baptism itself; for instance, the Pastoral Introduction to the service of Holy Baptism in *CW* includes several:

the sign of the cross, the badge of faith in the Christian journey, which reminds us of Christ's death for us. Our 'drowning' in the water of baptism, where we believe we die to sin and are raised to new life, unites us to Christ's dying and rising, a picture that can be brought home vividly by the way baptism is administered. Water is also a sign of new life, as we are born again by water and the Spirit, as Jesus was at his baptism. And as a sign of that new life, there may be a lighted candle, a picture of the light of Christ conquering the darkness of evil.

CW, p. 345

By employing these symbols, 'The service paints many vivid pictures of what happens on the Christian way' (*Common Worship*), and which are direct echoes of the biblical meanings.

Exercise

Consider the various New Testament images of baptism listed above. Which resonate most clearly with your own experiences?
How might you keep some of these images alive and ever-present in your church?

2

Baptism and the Journey of Faith

'We are all on a journey through life'

Common Worship: Pastoral Services, the Church of England's collection of liturgical resources for healing and wholeness, celebration of marriage, emergency baptism, thanksgiving for the gift of a child and ministries around death and bereavement begins with the statement 'We are all on a journey through life'. These services are intended to help us recognize the presence of God in the key points and crises of the human lifecycle: 'the journey we take is an accompanied one. God is with us every step of the way' (*Common Worship: Pastoral Services*, 1).

Much that is said about 'pastoral services' can also be said of baptism. It is important to note, however, that material for baptism is not collected together with the pastoral services in the *Common Worship: Pastoral Services* book, but it is to be found in the core book of the *Common Worship* with the Eucharist. More than a pastoral service, baptism is regarded as a 'gospel sacrament'. Number 25 of the Church of England's 39 Articles of Faith reads in part: 'there are two sacraments ordained by Christ our Lord in the Gospel, that is to say, Baptism, and the Supper of the Lord'. Furthermore, its presence in the core book of *Common Worship* points to the expectation that the ordinary context for baptism is in public worship, amid the gathered church.

Common Worship has more to say about journey in relation to the sacrament: 'Baptism marks the beginning of a journey with God for the rest of our lives, the first step in response to God's love' (*CW*, p. 345), and the introduction to the service mentions the journey motif four times. The words of the service itself also employ the image: for instance, parents and godparents are reminded, while making promises, that the children they bring are beginning a 'journey of faith' (*CW*, p. 352), and a prayer within the service speaks of God inviting the baptized one on 'a life-long journey' (*CW*, p. 359).

Stages on the way of faith

To fully understand the use of this journey imagery, it is important to learn something of the reforms to baptism that the Roman Catholic Church has undertaken since the Second Vatican Council 40 years ago, and from which the Protestant Churches have learned a great deal. Key to these Roman Catholic reforms was the *Rite of Christian Initiation of Adults (RCIA)*, published in 1978, and central to this is the role of catechesis (literally 'teaching pattern') over time.

The *RCIA* also uses the motif of 'journey' to describe its 'restoration, revision and adaptation' of the process by which the early (fourth-century) Church welcomed new believers, which we know from the sermons and writings that have come down to us from such important early Christian theologians as Cyril of Jerusalem and Ambrose of Milan. It is these writings that lie behind the third story at the start of this study. Based on the testimonies of early church luminaries, the *RCIA* highlights three essential steps towards baptism and aims to turn ancient practice into contemporary missionary activity:

* 'reaching the point of initial conversion and wishing to become Christians';
* progressing in faith through catechesis, teaching, and choosing a 'more intense' commitment;
* being spiritually prepared and so receiving the sacraments of baptism, confirmation and holy communion.
  Rite of Christian Initiation of Adults, Introduction, p. 3

Each of the steps involves public testimony and congregational celebration with the candidates, and crucially it all happens over time. The first two steps may last for several years, though the third step 'ordinarily coincides with the Lenten preparation for the Easter celebration'. Once initiated, there is then a further step: 'post-baptismal catechesis or mystagogy' – the name given to teaching and renewal *after* baptism. This mystagogy is understood as lasting a lifetime, and is consciously renewed every Lent and Easter as more new converts are welcomed, taught and baptized, and also engaged in evangelization at all times.

So that we can see how these ancient sources are used, here is an excerpt from a 'mystagogical' sermon by Cyril of Jerusalem, preached in the fourth century to the recently baptized:

> First you were anointed on the forehead so that you might lose the shame which Adam, the first transgressor, everywhere bore with him, so that you might 'with unveiled face behold the glory of the Lord' (2 Corinthians 3.18). Next you were anointed on the ears, that you might acquire ears which hear those divine mysteries of which Isaiah said: 'The Lord has given me an ear to hear with' (Isaiah 50.4). Again, the Lord Jesus in the gospel said: 'He who has ears, let him hear' (Matthew 11.15). Then you were anointed on the nostrils, so that after receiving the divine chrism you might say: 'We are the aroma of Christ to God among those who are being saved' (2 Corinthians 2.15). After that, you were anointed on the chest, so that 'having put on the breast-plate of righteousness, you might stand against the wiles of the devil' (Ephesians 6.14, 11). Just as Christ after his baptism and visitation by the Holy Spirit went out and successfully wrestled with the enemy, so you also, after your holy baptism and sacramental anointing, put on the armour of the Holy Spirit, confront the power of the enemy, and reduce it saying: 'I can do all things in Christ who strengthens me' (Philippians 4.13).
>
> Yarnold, *Awe-Inspiring Rites of Initiation*, pp. 83–4

The *RCIA* enacts this as a beautiful signing of the senses. First, the sign of the cross is traced over the catechumen's ears, with prayer that she 'may hear the voice of the Lord'. The signings are then made over different parts of the body: over the eyes, with prayer that the catechumen may see God's glory; over the lips, that she may respond to God's word; over the heart, 'that Christ may dwell there by faith'; over the shoulders, for strength to bear Christ's gentle yoke; over the hands, that Christ would be known in the catechumen's work; and finally over the feet, that she may walk in Christ's way. The whole person is embraced in an enacted prayer.

The *RCIA* claims to 'turn ancient practice' to 'contemporary missionary activity'. Do you think this works?

The *RCIA* has inspired Christians of other traditions to consider how contemporary baptismal liturgies can draw deeply on ancient roots. In each case, they are trying to facilitate the journey to faith, by staging and celebrating a number of points along the way. The churches have found that this has been especially important in helping adults come to faith, leading to adult baptism. The catechumenate is therefore seen as a crucial contemporary expression of mission.

The influence of the catechumenate is also to be felt in a number of contemporary evangelistic resources, which, like the catechetical process, tend to unfold over time. A clear example is the course *Emmaus – the Way of Faith*, which is popular in many Church of England parishes. Its subtitle points to the fact that Emmaus is 'a journey approach' to evangelism. *Emmaus* is consciously organized in three stages – contact, nurture and growth. And although these do not correspond to the four stages of the *RCIA* and now other churches' appropriations of the catechumenate, they do share some of its underlying emphases, notably:

- Entry into faith is a process of discovery.
- This process is best practiced as an accompanied journey.
- It is a process that affects the whole of our lives.
- Effective initiation affects the life of the whole church.
  Booker and Ireland, *Evangelism – Which Way Now?*, pp. 36–7

In fact, research shows that something like 69 per cent of British Christians testify that their own coming to faith was a gradual process, not least one that by their own estimates took on average four years.

Consider your own story of finding faith.
How long did it take/is it taking?
Has it involved some discernibly different 'stages'?
What insights does this suggest about teaching and learning in Christian faith?

3

Baptism and the Church's Mission

The welcome of the whole congregation

Most baptismal liturgies assume that the regular worshipping congregation is present to surround and support. The Church of England declares that baptism is 'normally' administered in the course of public worship on Sunday 'when the most number of people come together' (Canon B21). The 'pastoral introduction' to the service of baptism makes clear that the local church is envisaged as being present: 'the wider community of the local church and friends welcome the new Christian, promising support and prayer for the future' (*CW*, p. 345). And within the service of baptism itself, 'the whole congregation' is addressed and questioned as to whether they will both welcome and uphold those to be baptized in their new life in Christ. These are demanding challenges calling for both initial and ongoing hospitality and generosity from the congregation, who are invited to respond affirmatively.

Why is this important?

On this point there has been widespread ecumenical agreement: it is important to restore baptism to the Sunday assembly in order to make it clear that baptism is not just an infant blessing, a lifecycle rite affecting the baby and his or her immediate family, but an incorporation into the body of Christ. The wider community represents more adequately the entire body of Christ, the whole communion of saints, into which the child is being baptized. On the one hand, it is important for the baby's family and godparents to realize this larger community claims their child – both so that they may take seriously the communal nature of living the faith and so that they may experience the community's support in the task of rearing the child in the faith. On the other hand, it is necessary for the congregation to realize how it is implicated in the child's baptism, for *a rite of passage into a community is a rite of passage for the whole community.*

Ramshaw, 'How Does the Church Baptize Infants and Small Children?', p. 7

Ramshaw suggests that this translates as a challenge to congregations that might be expressed as: 'this is our new sister; you'd better get to know her, because you're responsible for her now'!

Exercise

How does your congregation 'welcome' and 'uphold' those baptized in your community? What might be done to offer better support to the baptized and their families?

Welcome at the Lord's table

Hospitality is also at the heart of the strong welcome many churches are now extending to children at the eucharist. The full participation of children in communion has broken the once common assumption that confirmation was necessary for admittance to holy communion. For example, the *Book of Common Prayer* (1662) suggested 'There shall none to be admitted to holy Communion, until such a time as he be confirmed, or be ready and desirous to be confirmed', and Cranmer's understanding, enshrined in the *BCP* of 1552, was stronger: 'There shall be none admitted to the holy Communion until such a tyme as he can saye the Catechisme, and bee confirmed.' Overturning these inherited viewpoints, the theological conviction now commonly expressed is:

Baptism is complete sacramental initiation and leads to participation in the eucharist. Confirmation and other rites of affirmation have a continuing pastoral role in the renewal of faith among the baptised but are in no way to be seen as a completion of baptism or as necessary for admission to communion.

Holeton, *Growing in Newness of Life*, p. 229

In this statement, the Anglican Communion has recently been facing the incongruous situation of having excluded baptized and believing children from its central act of worship. Rethinking the traditional pattern of baptism – confirmation – communion is itself often an expression of mission to young people, as well as requiring a more missionary orientation for confirmation. For if baptism is complete sacramental initiation, and confirmation is not the 'hoop' through which to jump to eucharist, a new role for confirmation is needed.

Exercise

What is the practice of your church in relation to children and communion? How do you ensure a welcome at the Lord's table for all?

Confirmation as commissioning to witness

Understanding and practice of confirmation across the Christian traditions is much more varied than that of baptism itself, and this is in part due to the widespread conviction that confirmation is 'a rite in search of a theology', not least in relation to scripture. According to *Walking in Newness of Life*, 'Confirmation affords those baptized as infants an opportunity to affirm, as adults, the faith of the Christian community into which they have been baptized' (Holeton, *Growing in Newness of Life*, p. 233). And some provinces of the Anglican Communion now tie the title 'confirmation' to 'commissioning'. In Kenya, for example, the service of confirmation and commissioning has candidates make a number of demanding pledges: to keep God's commandments; to read the scriptures and pray daily; to proclaim Christ; to live in fellowship with other Christians; to be active in the church community; to give to its good causes; to help the needy; to support the poor; and strive to be a good steward of God's gifts. Not only this, but to uphold truth and justice, and to seek reconciliation among all people. The service is clear that each of these things is part of the Church's mission, and that each of its members is commissioned to share in it.

Increasingly, throughout the Anglican Communion, the active embrace of mature Christian service is underscored in the rite. In *Common Worship*, these promises are found in the Confirmation service:

Will you continue in the apostles' teaching and fellowship,
in the breaking of bread and in the prayers?
With the help of God, I will.

Will you persevere in resisting evil, and
whenever you fall into sin, repent and return to the Lord?
With the help of God, I will.

Will you proclaim by word and example
the good news of God in Christ?
With the help of God, I will.

Will you seek and serve Christ in all people,
loving your neighbour as yourself?
With the help of God, I will.

Will you acknowledge Christ's authority over human society,
by prayer for the world and its leaders,
by defending the weak, and by seeking peace and justice?
With the help of God, I will.

Book of Common Prayer, 1979,
Episcopal Church in the USA

The strong ethical dimension of such questions is regarded as a recovery of the moral seriousness with which becoming a Christian was regarded in the early centuries:

In the first centuries of Christianity, seekers were required not just to profess their belief in Jesus as the Christ, but to make choices about their daily lives. The profession of Christian faith they would eventually be invited to make was not a matter merely of repeating doctrinal formulas, but was something to be tested in the crucible of daily life itself. Conversion of life was seen in how one related to others, in how one earned a living, in how one could be trusted.

Weil, *A Theology of Worship*, pp. 8–9

Exercise

Consider the expressions of commitment associated with confirmation, cited above. How do you respond to them?

4

Baptism and Christian Spirituality

We have seen that baptism relates us to Jesus, who was himself baptized, and in whose name we are baptized. Baptism is an invitation to discover ourselves as God's 'beloved'. It is an important stage on the way of faith, and a gracious invitation to journey through every circumstance of life with God. And as well as an invitation, baptism is a challenge: it challenges the Church in its mission, constantly calling the baptized to welcome yet more new members, both younger and older, and to testify to faith in their words and deeds. It is obvious, then, just how important it is that churches find ways to keep the images of baptism alive among their members, and that individuals constantly remember and celebrate baptism (their own and others!) to renew their sense of belonging in the community of the baptized. In this quest to help baptism matter to members of the churches, inspiration has been drawn from many sources. For example, Philip Pfatteicher writes of Martin Luther's baptismal spirituality:

No one has written more powerfully and eloquently of the eternal significance of baptism than Martin Luther. The principal glory of Lutheran theology is its profound understanding of the nature, power and duration of Holy Baptism. Baptism consists of preparation, presentation, thanksgiving, renunciation of evil and profession of faith in the triune God, baptism in water, laying on of hands and signation with the cross, welcome into the congregation and church, instruction in the mysteries of the faith, living, confessing and receiving forgiveness, dying, sharing in the resurrection. For, as Luther wrote in his gleaming essay *The Holy and Blessed Sacrament of Baptism* (1519), baptism is not fulfilled completely in this life. The physical baptism is quickly over, but the spiritual baptism, the drowning of sin, which it signifies, lasts as long as we live and is completed only in death.

Pfatteicher, *Liturgical Spirituality*, p. 241

Here, baptism is a way to live! The 'thanksgiving for holy baptism' in *CW* (pp. 48–50) might well be celebrated with Luther's words in mind.

Exercise

How, and when, might your congregation use this thanksgiving?

Enlarging the signs

The thanksgiving's rubric that 'water may be sprinkled over the people or they may be invited to use it to sign themselves with the cross' might also be enriched with the kind of ceremonial suggested in this lovely example from the Uniting Church in Australia:

An elder pours water into the font.
The elder then says:
Come, Lord Jesus,
refresh the lives of all your faithful people . . .

The minister may then say:
Today we remember that, from the time of our baptism,
the sign of the cross has been upon us.
I invite you now to join me
in tracing the sign of the cross upon your forehead,
saying – I belong to Christ. Amen.

The minister and the people may mark themselves with the sign, saying:
I belong to Christ. Amen.

The minister may also add:
You may trace the sign of the cross
on those around you,
saying – You belong to Christ. Amen.

The people may mark others with the sign, saying:
You belong to Christ. Amen.

Uniting in Worship, pp. 32–3 © Assembly of the
United Church of Australia, 1988. Used with permission

Richard Giles' recent work on 'transforming the liturgy of the eucharist', *Creating Uncommon Worship*, draws attention to the ways in which baptism can be remembered in each eucharistic event. He suggests that the Sunday assembly's invitation to repentance and absolution might be held at the font; for example, 'the people may come to the font one by one, to dip their finger in the water and to make the sign of the cross on themselves, or better still, make the sign on the cross on each other, as an interactive symbol of God's choosing and God's forgiveness'. Whatever form the penitential rite may take, above all Giles commends 'gathering at the well':

In many church buildings, to gather around the existing font is almost a practical impossibility, but do it nevertheless. Do it when only a few can get within touching distance, do it with people standing on pews or sitting on window sills. Do it until the cry goes up, 'How long, O Lord, how long . . . before we can build a proper font?' . . . Even the meanest, silliest, little bird bath, or the ugliest brute of a monster, can be a (temporary) reprieve if you take off (and lose) its lid, and fill it with water until it overflows . . .

Giles, *Creating Uncommon Worship*, pp. 100–2

This brings us to another important dimension in contemporary attempts to enliven the baptismal spirituality of Christian people. This is about enlarging both the vessels and gestures of baptism. 'A proper font', these days, might well consist of a pool large enough in which to submerge an adult, and employ the sound of running water, so that an audible echo of baptism is part of the liturgical environment as well as a stronger visible focus.

Exercise

How could your liturgies make better use of the baptismal symbolism of the font? How might the availability of more water help recover a sense of the joy of baptism? (Remember the babushkas!)

Conclusion

There is a pressing need to recover a sense of baptismal spirituality in order to link baptism and mission as well as to re-engage the challenge of accompanying the baptized on the journey of faith.

In this brief study, we have explored some contemporary understandings of baptism that have much to offer the church in its quest for a livelier sense of what baptism means. Here are some ideas based on the ground we have covered:

- Teach that faith is a journey; honour baptism as a stage on the way.
- Embrace the missionary imperative of baptism – welcome all who seek it, and find ways to accompany them over time.
- Work out what the model of the ancient catechumenate can offer to your own time and place as you invite seekers to grow into fuller appreciation and understanding of the faith.
- Celebrate baptism at the heart of the church – don't marginalize it; increase contact between seekers and assembly and challenge the congregation to gesture the hospitality it professes and for which it prays.
- Because of their baptism, include children fully in the eucharist; treasure them as members of the Church, not members-in-waiting.
- Revitalize confirmation; accentuate the responsibilities entailed.
- Enjoy the different images of baptism in scripture, especially those symbolized in the service itself; affirm the diverse experiences of grace that the range of symbols celebrate.
- Consider the possibility of enlarging the material signs of baptism – flowing water, lavish vessels, focal space . . .

- Above all, revisit baptism – and do so again and again; focus on the font in some way in every Sunday liturgy; constantly remember and refresh the sense of belonging to God through baptism.

In these ways, find ways to say in your community that baptism matters, that it affirms our central identity as God's beloved community, embraces us in the joy and pain of our journeys, and immerses us in a splendour that our liturgies struggle to express.

References and Further Reading

References in text

Baptism, Eucharist and Ministry, 1981, Geneva: World Council of Churches

Mike Booker and Mark Ireland, 2003, *Evangelism – Which Way Now?*, London: Church House Publishing

Common Worship: Pastoral Services, 2000, London: Church House Publishing

Common Worship: Services and Prayers for the Church of England, 2000, London: Church House Publishing

Richard Giles, 2004, *Creating Uncommon Worship: Transforming the Liturgy of the Eucharist*, Norwich: Canterbury Press

David R Holeton, ed., 1993, *Growing in Newness of Life: Christian Initiation in Anglicanism Today*, Toronto: Anglican Book Centre

Aidan Kavanagh, 1992, 'A Rite of Passage', Appendix 1, in Gabe Huck, *The Three Days: Parish Prayer in the Paschal Triduum*, Chicago, IL: Liturgy Training Publications, pp. 171–5

Modern Services, 1994, Nairobi: Uzima Press

John Patton, 1990, *From Ministry to Theology: Pastoral Theology and Action*, Nashville, TN: Abingdon Press

Philip Pfatteicher, 1997, *Liturgical Spirituality*, Valley Forge, PA: Trinity Press International

Elaine Ramshaw, 1995, 'How Does the Church Baptize Infants and Small Children?', in Gordon W Lathrop, ed., *What is Changing in Baptismal Practice?*, Minneapolis, MN: Fortress Press, pp. 6–13

Rite for the Christian Initiation of Adults: Study Edition, 1988, Chicago, IL:
Liturgy Training Publications
Colin Thubron, 2000, *In Siberia*, Harmondsworth: Penguin
Uniting in Worship, 1988, Melborne: Uniting Church Press
Louis Weil, 2000, *A Theology of Worship*, Cambridge, MS: Cowley
Edward Yarnold, 1994, The Awe-Inspiring Rites of Initiation: Origins of
the RCIA, Collegeville, MN: Liturgical Press, [2]

Further Reading

Thomas Best and Dagmar Heller, eds., 1998, *Becoming a Christian: The Ecumenical Implications of Our Common Baptism*, Geneva: WCC
David Holeton, ed., 1993, *Growing in Newness of Life: Christian Initiation in Anglicanism Today*, Toronto: Anglican Book Centre
Maxwell Johnson, ed., 2003, *Documents of the Baptismal Liturgy*, London: SPCK, [3]
Maxwell Johnson, 2001, *Images of Baptism*, Forum Essays no. 6, Chicago, IL: Liturgy Training Publications
Maxwell Johnson, ed., 1995, *Living Water, Sealing Spirit: Readings on Christian Initiation*, Collegeville, MN: Liturgical Press
Maxwell Johnson, 1999, *The Rites of Christian Initiation: Their Evolution and Interpretation*, Collegeville, MN: Liturgical Press
Aidan Kavanagh, 1978, *The Shape of Baptism: The Rite of Christian Initiation*, New York: Pueblo
Regina Kuehn, 1990, *A Place for Baptism*, Chicago, IL: Liturgy Training Publications
Liturgical Commission of the Church of England, 1995, *On the Way: Towards an Integrated Approach to Christian Initiation*, 1995, London: CHP
Jerome Overbeck, 1998, *Ancient Fonts, Modern Lessons*, Chicago, IL: Liturgy Training Publications
Gail Ramshaw, 1994, *Words Around the Font*, Chicago, IL: Liturgy Training Publications

Laurence Hull Stookey, 1982, *Baptism: Christ's Act in the Church*, Nashville, TN: Abingdon Press

World Council of Churches, 1981, *Baptism, Eucharist and Ministry*, Geneva: WCC

Edward Yarnold, 1994, *The Awe-Inspiring Rites of Initiation: The Origins of the RCIA*, Collegeville, MN: Liturgical Press, [2]